MARIA DA VILLA URBANI

The *BASILICA* of
SAINT MARK

and the *GOLD ALTARPIECE* - *120 Colour plates*

Gold Altarpiece
The Archangel
Michael.

Saint Peter confers the dignity of bishop on Saint Mark.
Between two cities Saint Peter bestows the Pastoral upon Saint Mark.
The cities are identical and are characterised
by a two-lighted arch-shaped window.

Aerial view of Saint Mark's Square (pages 2-3).

Gold Altarpiece

Doge Ordelaffo Falier (1102-18). The Doge's
garments are those of an imperial personality
while the head and the crown are later additions.

ST MARK'S:
THE DOGE'S CHURCH AND THE CITY'S CATHEDRAL

St Mark's basilica is a *martyrium* of the Evangelist saint, a reliquary church, a splendid "summa" of all the arts the Venetians concentrated here, in styles derived from both the East and the West over the centuries during which the city was a sovereign Republic. Over time St Mark's has lived two very important roles: that of the Palatine church or chapel of the ducal palace and, ever since 1807, that of the city's cathedral. The aerial photograph on the preceding pages clearly visualizes the entire "Marciana" area, the city core, and the buildings that make it up: the church, the palace, the square, the bell-tower, the old and new Procuratie, and the small square near the quay. The strong relationship between the church and the ducal palace, connected by means of simple interior passageways, and that between the church and the two squares are particularly evident (see photos pp. 24-25).

The doge, who was elected in the palace, would be presented to the town and publicly proclaimed from the "pergola" in St Mark's (the pulpit on the right reserved for the doge). From here he would enter the square and meet the people according to special rites and ceremonies (photo pp. 6-7). The doge

Gold sequin.
The figure of the Doge
kneeling in front of Saint Mark.

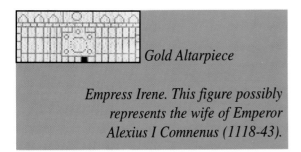

Gold Altarpiece

*Empress Irene. This figure possibly
represents the wife of Emperor
Alexius I Comnenus (1118-43).*

himself was the first celebrant of St Mark's, even though this role was covered in the liturgies by the "primicerius", the head of the basilica's clergy, who was nominated by the doge as his representative and granted episcopal prerogatives.

As the church of state, other official ceremonies similar to that of the presentation of the new doge were also performed in St Mark's, such as the benediction of the soldiers leaving for war or the presentation of captured enemy flags. The peace of Venice, the historical event that took place here in 1177, is still remembered by the names engraved on the marble flooring of the atrium, including the highest authorities of Europe such as Pope Alexander III, Emperor Frederick Barbarossa, and the doge of Venice, Sebastiano Ziani, promoter of the encounter.

In the beginning the space in front of the church was the "brolo" - vineyards, vegetable garden, fruit orchard - of the nuns of S. Zaccaria. It was bounded by Rio Batario, located around the middle of the present square, where the first church of S. Geminiano was set. During the late-twelfth century Doge Ziani decided to renovate what many centuries of history had by now granted: he purchased the "brolo", filled in the rio, and demolished the church of S. Geminiano. The latter was reconstructed, double its size, on the western border of the new square. The dock area near the quay was also filled. This is how the two square system was created: the space in front of the church defined one square; another was created between the bell tower, the foundations of which date back to the ninth century, and the palace, which was also transformed by the Doge.

The church, the third St Mark's, was further modified and enriched by the patient work of entire generations of artists commissioned by the government, which had entrusted the task of presiding over the basilica to the procurators of St Mark's *de supra*, one of the Republic's highest magistracies. The responsibility for overseeing building works and the con-

*Saint Mark presents Saint Hermagoras to Saint Peter.
The scene takes place inside the embattled walls of a town.
Saint Hermagoras dressed in white as a subdeacon; Saint Mark holds his
hand and presents him to Saint Peter. Saint Hermagoras
will be the founder of the Church of Aquileia.*

servation of monuments was given to the city's most prestigious architects, who assumed the title of "proto" or overseer of St Mark's (examples include Jacopo Sansovino in the 16th c. and Baldassare Longhena in the 17th c.). The entire "Marciana" complex reached its definitive organization over the course of the sixteenth century, through the work of Jacopo Sansovino (who designed the small loggia at the base of the bell tower and the library), and other great architects of the time, who interpreted the Doge's will for a grand revival capable of rebounding from the difficulties at the beginning of the century.

The church of St Mark's was also famous for its musical performances. The most important musicians of every age were requested by the Marciana chapel: Adrien Willaert, Claudio

Merulo, Andrea and Giovanni Gabrieli, Claudio Monteverdi, Giovanni Legrenzi, and Lorenzo Perosi. Music was played and sung from a multitude of places inside the church: not only in the two choirs at the sides of the presbytery, where the two famous organs were found, but also from the two small pulpit tribunes (attributed to Sansovino) located in front of the rood screen, as well as other places that took full advantage of the sonority of the basilica's space.

At the fall of the Serenissima Republic in 1797, the church of St Mark's had to accept the end of its centuries-long role as the palace chapel. Even the function of the "primicerius" and the ducal clergy, traditionally nominated by the doge from among the noble families, came to an end. Ten years later, in 1807, Napoleon ordered the patriarchal seat of San Pietro di Castello, a church situated at the extreme eastern end of the city near the sea, to be moved to St Mark's, and once again the church took on a vital role as the cathedral of Venice.

The neo-classical building on the small square to the north, the facade of which was realized by Lorenzo Santi between 1835 and 1850, was constructed as the living quarters of the patriarch. This title was reserved for the bishop of Venice from 1451 on when Lorenzo Giustiniani inherited it from the patriarchate of Grado, which in turn had received it from Aquileia, the city evangelized by St Mark. Over the course of our century, the importance of the patriarchal seat of Venice has been emphasised by the fact that three of its patriarchs were later elected popes of the universal church: Pius X (Giuseppe Sarto, 1835-1914, pope from 1903 to 1914), John XXIII (Angelo Giuseppe Roncalli, pope from 1903 to 1963), John Paul I (Albino Luciani, 1912-1978, pope for 33 days from 28 August to 29 September 1978).

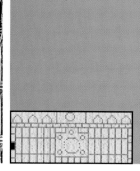

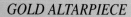

Healing of Anianus.
Near some town walls takes place the healing of Anianus
sitting at his cobbler bench on which you can see a knife
an awl, some leather and a shoe. Saint Mark
standing rushes to heal his left hand.

Atrium of the basilica.
The building of the Tower of Babel.

ST MARK EVANGELIST
AND VENICE

The first historical testimony about St Mark the Evangelist was recorded by Papias (135-201) bishop of Hierapolis in Asia Minor: "Mark, having become the interpreter of Peter, wrote in an exact, though not ordered way, everything he remembered of the things pronounced or achieved by the Lord. He did not listen to the Lord and was not his but, rather, a follower of Peter." Before this precise documentation, the Acts of the Apostles and the letters of Paul and Peter briefly recall Mark as their disciple and companion. (Peter is known to have referred to him as "my son".)

It is from these hints that the very ancient tradition of the eastern and of the western churches draws the origins of the tradition that identifies Mark as the spiritual son of Peter and considers him a writer of the Gospel (photo p. 9), which refers to the preaching of the prince of the Apostles.

In the Middle Ages the life of the saint was passed on in ancient tales, known as *Passiones*. Their literary form, with thes continuous references to biblical texts and in particular to the Gospels, was adapted to narrate the life of those who

CARNIB· ABSCONSV· VVERVNT FVGIVNTQ· RETRORSV·

The mosaics of Saint Mark's.
Presbytery, vault and south wall. East half of the vault.
Stories of Saint Mark. The translation of Saint Mark's body

Interior. Ascension Dome.
Saint Mark writing his Gospel.

adhered completely to the teaching of Jesus. The fundamental facts of Mark's life include his years as a disciple of Paul and Peter as they wandered about evangelizing, particularly in Africa and in Alexandria, Egypt, where he became bishop after being ordained by Peter in Rome, and finally his martyrdom on 25 April in 68.

Among the miracles St Mark performed in Alexandria the most well-known episode is the healing of Anianus, the cobbler. Having disembarked in Africa and reached the city of Alexandria, Mark tore his boot and entrusted its repair to a cobbler named Anasius, who he found working intently in his shop. Inadvertently, Anianus wounded his left hand with the awl. According to the medieval texts that recall the gestures of Jesus narrated by the Gospels, "Mark spit on the ground, made mud with his saliva" and spread it on the hand of the cobbler, who, upon the words "in the name of Jesus Christ be cured", was instantly healed. Anianus became Mark's disciple, and later his successor to the bishop's seat of Alexandria.

The cure of Anianus is portrayed more than once in the Marciana cycless of the basilica: in the mosaics, in the enamels of the Pala d'Oro (photo p. 8), in the Pala Feriale, and in the wooden

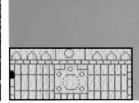

GOLD ALTARPIECE

Saint Mark destroys an idol.
The scene takes place near some town walls.
Saint Mark is seen while exorcising the idol atop a column.
The black idol is covered with armour and wears the helmet,
the lance and the sword. It is believed to represent Athena.

Galleries of the Academy.
Gentile Bellini:
the Procession of the Relic in Saint Mark's Square (1496).

Original project (conjectural)
of the main facade.
Water-colour by W. Scott from a drawing
by A. Pellanda. Second half of the 19th century.

marquetry of the sacristy. The evangelist tradition carried on by Peter's disciple spread to Aquileia, then to Grado, and finally, from the eighth century on, to the Veneto lagoon around the newly-emerging city of Venice. After being ordained bishop in Rome by Peter, Mark is said to have reached Aquileia, where he performed some miracles, baptized the faithful, and chose a young nobleman, Hermagoras, to take with him to Rome to be ordained by Peter. He later became the first bishop of Aquileia, from where the entire subsequent Venetian patriarchal tradition began.

In 828 two Venetian merchants, Bonus from Malamocco and Rusticus from Torcello, disembarked in Alexandria of Egypt. On their way to venerate the reliquaries of St Mark in the church where they were preserved, they learned that, precisely in those days, the Christian church was to be destroyed to make room for the construction of mosques. To save the Saint's body from profanation, they decided to move it to the very city he had evangelized (photo p. 9). The adventurous trip from Alexandria to Venice concluded happily and the saint, by now patron of the Venetian Republic, was protected.

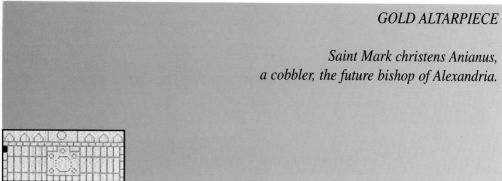

*Saint Mark christens Anianus,
a cobbler, the future bishop of Alexandria.*

Gold Altarpiece.
Mary praying. The Virgin, in the act of praying as far as style is concerned
links up to the Empress Irene and the Doge. This figure corresponds to other
similar Byzantine representations of the 11th and 12th Cent.

The basilica viewed from the Clock-tower
(pages.14-15).

The Venetian version of the Stories of St Mark was enriched with
details over time (the most well-known is Mark's dream during his
journey to the lagoons, in which an angel pointed out his future resting place). They are widely illustrated by the mosaics on the choirs at
the sides of the presbytery (12th c.), on the vault of the Zen chapel
(13th c.), and on the lunettes of the facade (see p. 31).
A very beautiful thirteenth-century mosaic panel in the south transept
narrates the miracle of *the recovery of St Mark's body* from inside a
pilaster of the basilica. Indeed, the record of where the doge and the
"primicerius", by then deceased, had hidden the Saint's body to avoid
its theft or profanation had been lost during the long eleventh-centu-
ry construction. The two scenes of the mosaics depict its miraculous
rediscovery in images of the basilica's interior - its five domes, the
vaults, the large arches, the arches resting on pilasters, the three pul-
pits (both single and double) - that narrate the prayers of invocation
and thanksgiving by the doge, the patriarch and its clergy, the nobles,
and the people (cover photo).

Plan of the basilica and of principal mosaic cycles

1	*Presbytery*
2	*Presbytery dome (Emmanuel)*
3.4	*Arches of the Presbytery*
	Right arch of the Presbytery
	Stories of St Mark
5	*Central dome (Ascension)*
6	*North arm dome (St John's dome)*
7	*Chapel of St Isidore*
8	*North transept arch*
9	*West arch of the central dome (Passion arch)*
10	*Arch with stories of Christ*
11	*South arm dome (St Leonard's dome)*
12-13	*Arches of St Leonard's dome*
14	*Entrance dome (Pentecost)*
15	*Left nave*
16	*Right nave*
17	*Main internal Portal*
I	*Atrium. The Genesis small dome*
II	*Atrium. Small dome with stories of Abraham*
III-IV-V	*Atrium. Small domes with stories of Joseph*
VI	*Atrium. Small dome with stories of Moses*
VII	*Atrium. Zen chapel*
VIII	*Baptistry*

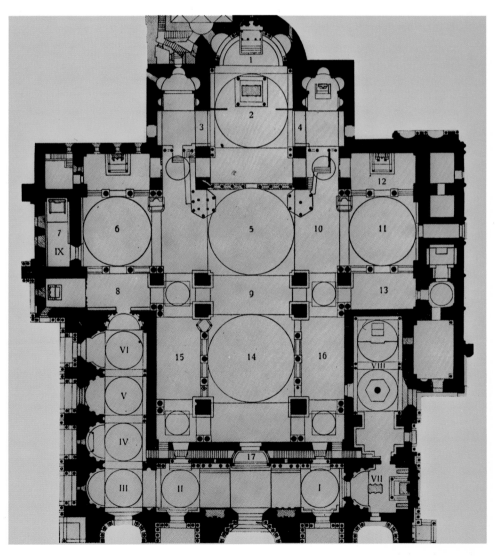

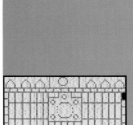

GOLD ALTARPIECE.

Apparition of Christ to Saint Mark.
The scene takes place inside some town walls between Christ,
isolated by a strip of white-dotted sky, and a meek-looking
Saint Mark, dressed in a tunic. The plaque shows the engraved
words that became the motto of the Venetian Republic:
Pax tibi, Marce, evangelista meus
(Peace be with you, Mark my Evangelist).

FUNDAMENTAL DATES
OF THE BASILICA

West facade, fourth
portal. Detail

The domes of St Mark's

829. Translation of St Mark's body from Alexandria in Egypt to Venice (Doge Giustiniano Partecipazio);

832. Consecration of the first church of St Mark's (Doge Giovanni Partecipazio);

976-978. Fire in the church because of the revolt against Doge Candiano IV and its rebuilding under Doge Candiano Orseolo I the Saint;

1063. Beginning of the building of the present church (Doge Domenico Contarini);

1071-1084. Beginning of mosaic decoration (Doge Domenico Selvo);

1094. Consecration of the church (Doge Vitale Falier);

1159. Beginning of marble panelling (Doge Vitale Michiel II);

1204. 4th Crusade and transfer into basilica of marbles and works of art filched following conquest of Constantinople (4 horses, icon of Madonna Nicopeia, enamels of Gold Altarpiece, reliquaries, crosses, goblets, paterae now in the Treasury). (Doge Enrico Dandolo);

1265. Mosaic of St Alypius with documentation of exterior of basilica;

1343-1354. Building of Baptistry and Chapel of St Isidore (Doge Andrea Dandolo):

1394. Building of iconostasis and sculptures decorating it by Jacobello and Pier Paolo dalle Masegne (Doge Antono Venier).

End 14th and early 15th Cent. Gothic decoration of facade with cusps, aedicules, sculptures of angels and saints;

1419. Fire on front part of basilica roof.

First half of 15th Cent. Work of Tuscan artists (Maestro Nicolò and Pietro Lamberti, possibly Jacopo della Quercia) in sculptures of facade; Florentine artists in mosaics of basilica (Paolo Uccello documented in 1425).

Half way through 15th Cent. Mosaic ornamentation of Chapel of the Mascoli;

1486. Building of Sacristy beside apse (to which follows rebuilding of the little church of St Theodore to order of Giorgio Spavento, overseer);

1496. Documentation of exterior of basilica in picture by Gentile Bellini *"Procession in St Mark's Square"*;

1504-1521. Building of Zen Chapel in right arm of atrium, building which closed off the solemn cntrance portal towards the lagoon;

1529. Intervention of Sansovino for strengthening of walls and of the domes of the church;

1617. Arrangement of Nicopeia altar and altar of Holy Sacrament (to lelt and right of main altar);

1797. Fall of the Republic;

1807. The basilica becomes seat of the Patriarch of Venice which, till then, had been at St Peter's in Castello.

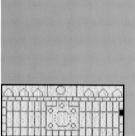

*Saint Mark is dragged into jail.
Saint Mark is inside a church in front of the altar
while above two guards wearing bizarre hats tighten
a noose around his neck. It is not clear whether the
Saint is being martyrized or taken into jail.*

ST MARK'S CHURCH
DOWN THE CENTURIES

The building begun by Giustiniano Partecipazio, the doge who received St Mark's body upon its arrival in Venice in 828, and finished by his brother and successor Giovanni was certainly completely different from St Mark's as we know it. Indeed scholars have yet to confirm its exact size and structure, and in the absolute absence of ancient documents, research and studies of the last one hundred years have suggested different hypotheses for the **first church of St Mark's**. It could have been built on a Latin basilica plan like the churches of Ravenna (and would have covered the perimeter of the present major nave), or on a Latin cross plan with two short transepts, or, finally, on a central plan with a dome over the sepulchre of St Mark (at the centre), within the perimeter of the present day crypt. The latter hypothesis is now the most widely accepted, especially after the recent crypt restoration which has made it possible to better observe the ancient walls. This would further verify the frequent reference made in ancient chronicles to the model of the Holy Sepulchre in Jerusalem.

Tradition later mentions a **second church of St Mark's** constructed by Pietro Orseolo I, who succeeded Candiano IV, the doge killed in the palace conspiracy of 976, when the fire in the ducal palace spread to and partially destroyed the southwestern corner. Today, it is common opinion among scholars that the church restored at this time was that of the Partecipazi, rather than a new building.

In the eleventh century the precise political will of the Government led to the decision to erect a new, completely renovated

and considerably enlarged building that most certainly encompassed the precedent foundations and parts of the wall structure. By then a great marine power, Venice's most powerful impulse to realize **the third St Mark's** was probably political pride, particularly at a time when a great number of Italian cathedrals were being constructed or rebuilt, including that of Pisa, Venice's antagonist.

According to ancient chronicles, the church was begun in 1063, under the rule of Doge Domenico Contarini. In 1071 Doge Domenico Selvo received the ducal investiture in the "*nondum perfecta* - not yet finished" church; the basilica was consecrated in 1094, under the rule of Doge Vitale Falier, who is buried in the atrium.

The original cross plan with five large domes, one for each arm of the cross and one at the centre, was modelled after the very well-known *Apostoleion* of Constantinople, the sixth-century church of the Twelve Apostles, destroyed in the fifteenth century when the Turks conquered Constantinople. The sustaining structure of each dome defines a precious underlying space: four large vaults resting on four pilasters, the interior of each of which repeats, almost in miniature, the dome-vault-pilaster model. What is apparently fragmentary in the nature of the spatial elements in reality gives the interior a solemn sense of unitary space. The upper part, covered by the golden "skin" of the mosaics in which the precious icons of the history of Christian salvation are set, continues to communicate to faithful followers and visitors alike the ancient symbolic meaning of

Main portal, arches.
The tunning of wine.

Main portal, arches.
The butcher

heaven or the divine space hovering over the underlying earth (photo p. 47).

The church was structurally completed in the late-eleventh century and its large domes and vaults inlaid with mosaics over the course of the twelfth. Over time, adjustments and additions were made: some were of an architectural character (the 12th c. atrium, the baptistry, and the chapel of St Isidore, the 15th c. Mascoli chapel, the Zen chapel, and the 16th c. sacristy); others were sculptural and mosaic in nature. As far as the exterior is concerned, the completion of the church is well documented in Giovanni Bellini's large canvas of 1496 (photo pp. 10-11).

The **marble facing** of the interior, which covers the lower part of the walls, is enriched by the vertical marble slabs, the coloured veining of which forms very beautiful, fanciful designs, following natural geometries. To the modern visitor their effect seems to be simply that of elegant and refined tapestries placed along the walls. Yet to Albert the Great

-a thirteenth-century philosopher, theologian and naturalist, who saw and was fascinated by stone-cutters preparing the characteristic marble slabs for the wall facing - the two open faces of a split slab that was to be placed alongside the others on the walls of the ducal church contained "the figure of a king with a crowned head and a long beard". The passage in which this observation is found helps us understand the techniques with which the marble facing was executed, yet it also expresses, in a very evocative way, how men of the Middle Ages could read a wealth of meanings in the most inert materials.

Set, like precious stones, within these beautiful marbles are numerous sculpted slabs of various provenance and dates. A journey through them immediately emphasises a theme very dear to the Venetians: devotion to the Madonna. Her image is repeated many times beginning from the walls at the side of the two lateral doors. Near the door of St Peter, to the left of the central portal, in a gilded thirteenth-century bas-relief, *the Vir-*

19

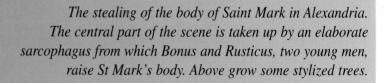

*The stealing of the body of Saint Mark in Alexandria.
The central part of the scene is taken up by an elaborate
sarcophagus from which Bonus and Rusticus, two young men,
raise St Mark's body. Above grow some stylized trees.*

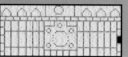

*Lunette above the central portal.
The Deesis (Mary and St. Mark's prayer
of intercession with Jesus).*

*View of the vault between the Ascension and
Pentecost domes.*

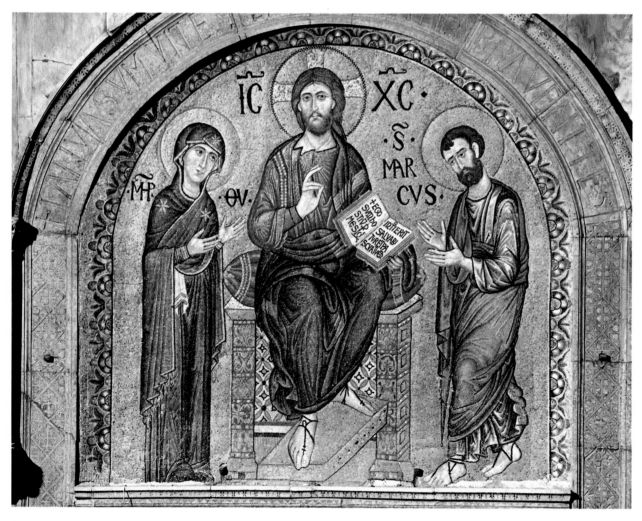

The translation of Saint Mark's body. On the stylized sea, with wheel-like waves, runs a sailing-ship shoved by the wind, and the sails wear the symbols of Christianity.

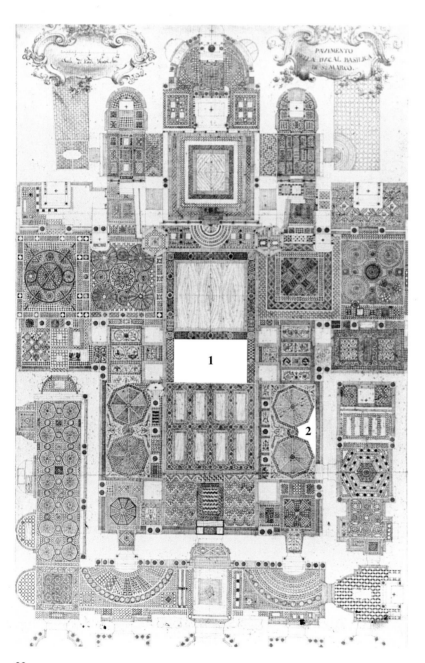

Plan of the mosaic floor of the basilica. The white section (n.1) corresponds to the enlarged detail on facing page. Mosaics made of opus tessellatum *and* opus sectile. *The second one, in* opus tessellatum, *is on page 62-63.*

gin (of the Graces), her hands lifted in prayer, is worshipped with devotion and candles are still lit for her supplicated protection. Near the door of St Clement, to the right of the portal, Mary and St John the Baptist are found at the sides of Christ in a classical *Deesis* of very ancient Byzantine provenance: these two greatest intercessors address a prayer to Christ the Redeemer, in the name of all men.

At the centre of the church, at the intersection with the left transept, one notes a large slab sculpted with the figure of Mary with a gun at her side: this is the so-called *Virgin of the "schioppo"* (gun). This particular ex-voto seems to have been offered by the Veneto Marines, miraculously saved after the

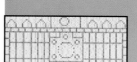

GOLD ALTARPIECE

Translation of Saint Mark's body into the basilica. It is a very evocative scene based on the two young Venetian merchants, Bonus and Rusticus, who carry the body, and a boy, who seems to express joy for the event in his physical attitude. Behind is a group of soldiers while in front the clergy with a cross and the thurible are waiting to enter the basilica.

Saint Mark's "Piazzetta" (small square) viewed from the roof of the basilica.

Saint Mark's Square viewed from the roof of the basilica.

explosion of an Austrian bomb in Marghera in 1849. Then, at the intersection with the right transept, there is the well-known *Virgin of the Kiss,* worn by the ancient custom of the faithful who express their devotion to Mary by kissing her half-bust statue with the Child. Francesco Saccardo defines this work "the most beautiful of the Byzantine Madonnas of St Mark's". The greatest number of slabs sculpted with the image of Mary are concentrated around the chapel of the north transept dedicated to St John the Evangelist and to the Virgin, of whom the mosaics "speak" at length. Indeed the Nicopeia Madonna, set in its precious silver frame with ancient enamels, stones, and pearls, found its definitive place here inside the new Baroque altar in 1618. This icon, which tradition numbers among those painted by St Luke, reached Venice from Constantinople after 1204. Painted on wood, it portrays the Virgin in a frontal half-bust, holding the Child in front of her breast, an almost "osten-

sory" Madonna. The title, Nicopeia or carrier of victory, suggests the special protection the Byzantine imperial troops originally asked of this icon. The Nicopeia Madonna has always been highly venerated in Venice, and according to ancient chronicles, this precious icon, conserved above the sacristy before 1618, was only shown to the public on the occasion of great celebrations or famous processions (photo p. 80). Among the basilica's numerous sculptural elements from various eras those situated in the area of the presbytery, the privileged space for liturgical celebrations, deserve particular attention.

The **ciborium,** which covers the high altar above St Mark's tomb, is made up of a block of stone in precious green Eastern marble, sustained by four, thirteenth-century (?) sculpted columns in calcareous alabaster. The reliefs of the columns, placed on nine registers each of which is overlaid by a gilded

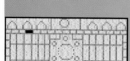

GOLD ALTARPIECE

Annunciation
The scene takes place in Mary's house
between Archangel Gabriel raising
his hands in blessing and the Virgin.

(Pages 28-29)
Marciano Museum.
The four Horses.

The main Portal with
the sculpted Arches (13th cent.).

inscription, narrate the life of the Virgin and of Jesus according to the story of the Gospels, with particular passages from the Revelations (photo p. 53).

The Gothic **rood screen** by Pierpaolo and Jacobello dalle Masegne (1394) is a transenna of coloured marbles that separates, in Eastern style, the presbytery (reserved for the clergy) from the nave (occupied by the faithful). At the top, at the sides of the central Crucifix, there are fourteen very beautiful statues portraying the twelve apostles, the Virgin, and St Mark (photo p. 51).

The credit for the sixteenth-century bronze masterpieces in the presbytery goes to Jacopo Sansovino, overseer of St Mark's: the very beautiful door that leads to the sacristy (photo p. 77), inspired by the doors of the baptistry in Florence; the small tabernacle door of the altar of the Sacrament with the withered Christ upheld by two angels; the four evangelists on the balusters; and the eight panels with the stories of St Mark in the two small tribunes near the rood screen, used as choirs in ancient times.

Last of all, **the flooring** is an important part of the interior marble facing. Like many other aspects of the basilica's decoration, it melds elements of classical iconography common to the Upper Adriatic area with others of Byzantine influence. Those of the former include the wheels, squares, hexagons, and octagons; the cornices decorated with circles and rhombi; the images of animals (photo p. 23 and pp. 62-63) and of figures entwined in vine branches - each of which takes on a par-

ticular meaning within the rich medieval Christian symbolism. The latter include the eight large slabs in Greek marble at the foot of the cross and another twelve below the cupola of the Ascension (photo p.47) with, in the words of Francesco Sansovino, "spots that resemble the movement of a wavy sea, for which the marble is in fact named".

The general plan of the flooring, perhaps already realized by the twelfth century, is well-inserted into the architecture and reveals a unitary approach, almost like a great oriental rug spread out over the base of the building. The highly coloured marbles are done in the *opus sectile* technique, in which patterns are realized with small pieces of marble of various shapes and sizes. This technique was used more frequently than that of the *opus tessellatum* in which the marble pieces are all the same size, though, here, the two techniques are integrated (photo pp. 62-63). Small parts of the ancient mosaics can be found spread out a bit everywhere among the many replacements that resulted from the fragility of the materials and the use to which the pavement has been and is constantly exposed. Some of the inlays - including some of the prospective rosettes near the door of St Peter and inside the church - are rightly attributed to the Florentine painter Paolo Uccello, whose presence in Venice is documented in 1425.

The first complete pavement design is the celebrated panel realized in pen by Antonio Visentini (photo p 22), which is part of the illustrative material of the basilica's history published in 1761 by Antonio Zatta.

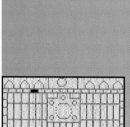

Portal and lunette of Saint Alypius.
The translation of Saint Mark's body into the basilica.
A 1265 ca. mosaic with the description of what
the facade was like in those days.

THE FACADES

The hypothetical reconstruction of the original western facade (photo p.11) shows how the exterior of St Mark's was resolved in Western-Romanesque building modules. The apses of the church (though largely incorporated in the structure of the ducal palace and the rectory houses) and the southern transept (adjacent to the palace courtyard and visible from the piazzetta) are still a splendid document of this kind of building.

A nineteenth-century restoration of the facade marbles made it possible to verify that the facing had been added at a later date. Indeed, the bricks of the niches found underneath the stone slabs were rounded off and regularly arranged just as they would have been had they been intended to be visible. A few fragments of very ancient mosaics were also brought to light. After the 1204 conquest of Constantinople, the Venetians were able to display a large quantity of precious Eastern marbles, columns, and capitals that had belonged to sacred and secular buildings of the Eastern Roman capital. The three facades were subsequently embellished with these marble slabs, columns, and capitals, into which gilded mosaics were set like enamels. The first period of decoration done by Venetian artists with the imported Early Christian or Byzantine materials, along with that which was partially renovated or completely new, was carried out during the thirteenth century.

What follows is an attempt to view these mosaics and marbles in light of their spiritual message, which the exterior of the church already intended to evoke in faithful followers and visitors.

Mosaics were widely inserted into the **main facade**. Starting from the underside of the first arch above the right doorway, one finds the portrayal of the *Removal of St Mark's body* by the Venetians Bonus (from Malamocco) and Rusticus (from Torcello) in 828 from Alexandria, Egypt, where the Saint had been buried after his martyrdom (done by an unknown mosaic artist on cartoons by Pietro Vecchia, c. 1660). Towards the left, above the other doorways are the *Arrival of St Mark's body in Venice* (also by an unknown mosaic artist on cartoons by Pietro Vecchia, c. 1660), the *Veneration of the body by the Doge and the Signoria* (by the mosaic artist Leopoldo Dal Pozzo on cartoons by Sebastiano Ricci, 1728-29), and the *Procession carrying the Saint into the basilica* (13th c.). The mosaics of the lower order celebrate the presence of St Mark's relics in Venice and the Basilica, which reassured the Venetians of their faith in Christ, based, according to tradition, on the preaching of Mark the Evangelist and, at the same time, guaranteed Venice as a free and just city, and a source of civilization.

Continuing and completing our vision are the four lunettes of the upper order where, from left to right, one finds the final

mysteries of the life of Jesus: *death, descent into limbo, resurrection, ascension* (photo pp.34-35). All of these mosaics were redone by Luigi Gaetano based on cartoons by Maffeo Verona (1617-18). In the centre, above the entrance, is the eschatological vision of the *last coming of Christ the Judge*. This is the basilica's last mosaic, done by Liborio Salandri on cartoons by Lattanzio Querena (1836-38) (photo p. 27).

Seen in their entirety, these works carry the message of salvation brought by Jesus to mankind, and preached in the lagoon by Mark the Evangelist. They are a taste of what is developed more fully on the large domes, vaults, walls, and undersides of the arches of the church's interior.

This unitary mosaic series is documented in its original thirteenth-century version in Gentile Bellini's large canvas from 1496, portraying the *Procession of the Cross in St Mark's Square* (photo pp.10-11). Today, all that remains of these ancient mosaics are those in the cove above the door of Saint Alypius, which depict the Translation of the body of St Mark into the Basilica (photo p.29). The others, done during the seventeenth and eighteenth centuries, respect and repeat the ancient iconography, according to the regulations set forth by Procurators of St Mark's, which required mosaicists to substitute ruined or partial mosaics with the original subject and inscription. Numerous other smaller mosaics depict solitary figures of saints, which are represented on the main as well as the two side facades. St Christopher is found among them, inside the left niche on the south facade in the direction of the quay.

Depicted crossing the impetuous river with baby Jesus on his shoulder, the image of St Christopher is common on the facades of many ancient churches because of its apotropaic meaning. The saint, who is frescoed in a famous execution by Titian located in the ducal palace above a door of the doge's apartment, is repeated in a statue on the north facade and in a

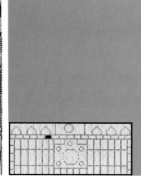

Presentation at the temple.
Under a canopy the Virgin presents the Child to
Simeon. Behind the Virgin Saint Joseph
offers two doves and behind Simeon,
Anne is seen with an open scroll.

mosaic in the atrium. The brief inscription found on the latter renders explicit the reasons for the widespread devotion to this saint: *"Christophori sancti faciem quicumque intuetur illo namque die nullo languore tenetur;* whoever looks at the image of St Christopher will not be struck by evil on that day." In ancient times the "sea-door" opened below the mosaic of St Christopher on the south facade. For a certain period of time, this was the most important entrance to the basilica because it was the closest to the palace and because it permitted direct access from the quay, the ancient "door" of the city. The underside of the thirteenth-century arch is sculpted with figures of prophets and a large eagle (at the top), symbol of resurrection and life, emphasize the symbolic meaning every entrance held for the congregation as it passed into the sacred space of the church.

On the south facade there are many marble elements, almost all of which are from Constantinople. The most famous are the porphyry Tetrarch group at the corner of the Treasury and the so-called acritani or square pillars of Acre, the origin of which recent archeological discoveries have definitively and precisely determined to be Byzantium, and not St John of Acre as had been commonly believed.

Whether the marble is spread out, used in single sculpted slabs as in the lower stone facing or the door surrounds, or, lastly, in the crowning of the upper fastigium, the message that comes from it privileges those of the main facade, where three nuclei of great interest can be identified.

The Byzantine slabs set in the thirteenth century should be viewed as counterparts starting from the main portal. The two warrior saints, St George and St Demetrius protect the entrance from evil and, by extension, from all enemies. The next slab on the left depicts the archangel Gabriel, while that on the right portrays the Virgin; together they represent the scene of the annunciation.

It is well-known that this Christian holiday (25 March) has always been remembered, from the earliest Venetian chronicles on, as the date the city was founded in 421. "In ditto zorno la verzene Maria fo annonciata da l'angel Cabriel.... era zorno de grande cerimonia et cusì i nostri progenitori volsero ellezer ditto zorno a tal e tanta edificatione": this is how Marin Sanudo the younger recalls the founding of the city in his chronicle from the late-fifteenth century. And this is why the calendar of the Veneto began the year in the month of March. It is also why the scene of the annunciation was sculpted and painted numerous times throughout the city (one example may be found on the west side of the Rialto bridge).

Finally, we come to the two slabs at the extremities of the facade depicting the labours of Hercules. Here we are indebted to Erwin Panofsky for a correct interpretation of these pagan scenes employed on the facade of a Christian church. "The Middle Ages" he writes "were not at all blind to the visual values of classical art and were profoundly interested in the intellectual and poetic values of classical literature. It is significant that, at the height of the mediaeval period... in Italian and French art of the twelfth and

South wall of the
Pentecost dome.
The Prayer
in the Garden
of Olives.

thirteenth century, we find a great number of pagan themes that are transformed into Christian themes." The two representations of Hercules on the facade of St Mark's – Hercules bringing King Eurystheus the monstrous wild boar from Mount Erymanthus, a slab of Byzantine origin from the Theodosian era (at the extreme left) and the thirteenth-century representation of Hercules killing the hydra infesting the swamps of Lerna, near Argos (at the extreme right) – transform "the mythological story into an allegory of Christian salvation".

Unlike the precedent imported slabs, the sculptures on the undersides of the arches bordering the central doorway constitute a *unicum* (photo p.27), a masterpiece by thirteenth-century Venetian artists, who were trained in the Byzantine school and gradually opened to Western, Paduan, and French influences. On the interior bands and on the frontal pieces sacred and profane themes intertwine, with some specific Venetian details. The undersides of the second and third arches are particularly outstanding for their extraordinary beauty. The former portrays personifications of the months of the year and the respective zodiac signs (in the intrados, readable from left-January to right-December), and seventeen female figures placed on pedestals and foliage of vines and pomegranates that personify the virtues and beatitudes (on the front). The third arch presents the crafts (in the intrados) with fisherman and squeraroli (Venetian boatmakers) placed next to the activities common to other cities (butchers and coopers, photo p.19), and (on the front at the sides of Christ Emmanuel) seven male figures representing the prophets and one female figure, perhaps a sibyl, who, according to a recent interpretation by Guido Tigler, "witness" the

divinity of Christ and his central position in the history of mankind as well as here in Venice.

The third nucleus is composed by the Gothic crowning, done between the fourteenth and the fifteenth century by Tuscan artists (the presence of Nicolò and Pietro Lamberti and Giovanni di Martino da Fiesole has been documented). It is an ensemble of 'inhabited' niches, statues and decorative volutes.

The ancient scene of the annunciation is repeated inside the niches found at the extremities: the angel Gabriel kneels on the left, the Virgin on the right. They constitute the base of an ideal arch with the statue of St Mark at its peak and the four evangelists and their symbols inside (Matthew-angel, Mark-lion, John-eagle, Luke-bull).

Below each there is a gargoyle in the form of a man, from which the rain water collected in the roof gutters drains. In ancient times, according to Francesco Sansovino, this water was collected "by a few occult channels" and, through a series of filters, made drinkable for Venetians. Evident here is the symbolic link between the water and its vital function and the word carrying the new life of the Gospels, which were destined to irrigate the earth. Four other gargoyles are located on the crowning of the **north facade** under the statue of the Fathers of the Western church: Ambrose, Augustine, Jerome, Gregory the Great. They represent the tradition that gathered, preserved, and passed on the word of the Gospel. Even the water that carried their names was considered salutary for Venice and a source of life.

On the north facade one can also admire the marble inlays of various origins, as well as the arch over the **door of the Fiori** (Flowers), which depicts the nativity in Byzantine forms in an extraordinary exam-

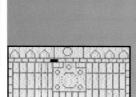

The Baptism of Christ.
Christ is immersed in the Jordan embodied by a human
figure holding a cup from which water is flowing.
At Christ's sides, the Baptist, a tree and an Angel,
in the centre the Holy Ghost in the form
of a dove, and two Angels on the right.

ple of thirteenth-century Venetian sculpture. Above the "flamboyant" arches where, amidst rich foliage, the half busts of the prophets seem to well-illustrate verse 13 of psalm 91 *"iustus ut palma florebit* - the just will blossom like a palm", the warrior saints (this time in four) reappear in their protective role on the main facade. The three theological virtues (faith, hope, charity) and the four cardinal (justice, prudence, fortitude, temperance) are depicted on the two minor facades.

From the top of the most important arch, St Mark blessing dominates the square and the city. Rising toward him are the incense-bearing angels, expressing the honour and devotion of all Venetians. At the centre of the star-studded mosaic below one finds the lion with the open book and the inscription: *"Pax tibi Marce Evangelista meus:* Peace to you St Mark, my Evangelist.

Finally, on the loggia, appear the pawing horses of St Mark's, the only example of **a quadriga** in existence. It was placed here when it reached Venice after 1204, along with the war spoils from the victory at Constantinople. The mosaic in the cove of the Sant'Alipio portal, dated around 1265, is its first testimony. The will of Venice - then an economically and politically emerging state - to consider itself heir to the glory and the name of Rome and the new Eastern Rome (Constantinople), prompted the aging Doge Enrico Dandolo to move the horses from the hippodrome in Byzantium to Venice. The Marciana quadriga remained charged with glory for the city, for the doge who appeared before it from the loggia, and for St Mark. Francesco Petrarch testified to this in a letter of 1364 written to a friend in Bologna: "One sees ... the four gilded bronze horses whose ancient craftsman has given them such a semblance of life, you almost seem to hear them pawing and whinnying." The descriptive liveliness of this passage is very interesting and suggests the emblematic and symbolic value of the liberty and power attributed to the quadriga.

Napoleon, too, was aware of this, and, at the fall of the Venetian Republic, he had the horses of St Mark's taken to Paris to celebrate his triumphs. They were returned to the basilica loggia immediately after 1815. Today, in order to avoid altering the secular iconography of the facade, copies have substituted them, and the originals, restored during the 1970s, are jealously conserved in the

The north Facade.

Marciano Museum, where they can still be long admired in the integrity of their vigorous beauty (photo pp. 28-29). The bronze gates were inserted between the thirteenth and fourteenth century, during the realization of the facade's marble facing (photo p. 16). The Venetian goldsmith Bertuccio, who signed the second gate on the left in 1300, imitated the decorative motif and small arches of the beautiful **central portal**, perhaps from sixth-century Constantinople, adapted here to ennoble the main entrance to the church (photo p. 27). Its two wings are constituted by bronze transennas decorated with thirty-four lines of small arches, in the form of a fan or peacock's tail (*opus clatratum*), according to the motifs present in both classical and early-Christian art.

Finally, one of the elements that characterizes the church's exterior profile are the thirteenth-century domes, born of the need to enlarge the building after the reconstruction and enlargement of the square and the ducal palace under the rule of Doge Sebastiano Ziani. In their realization, this practical need was not separated from the distant fascination of the domes of Eastern churches and mosques, so-well known to Venetian merchants and to crusaders that passed through Venice.

The domes (photo p. 17), whose very complex structure of horizontal and vertical wooden elements is a masterpiece of Venetian carpentry, are covered with sheets of lead. Small cupolas, the form of which varies for each dome, rise above, topped by a cosmic cross, the arms of which, turned to the four cardinal points, terminate in gilded spheres.

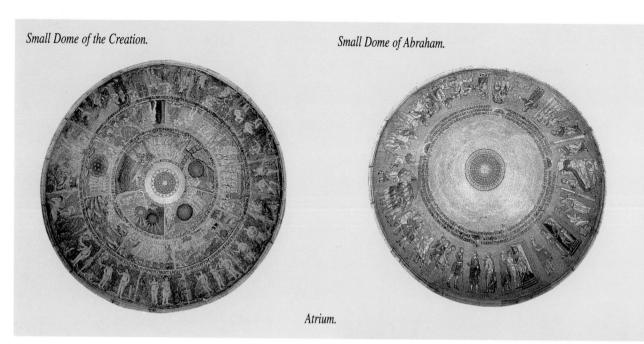

Small Dome of the Creation.

Small Dome of Abraham.

Atrium.

MOSAICS OF THE ATRIUM

To enter the church from the square one must pass through the atrium, which was added to the Contarini building complex in the late-twelfth century and decorated over the course of the thirteenth with the mosaics that cover the cupolas, vaults, and lunettes. These works are the mature expression of a completely Venetian laboratory of mosaicists and testify to the stylistic evolution that took place over the span of approximately sixty years during which the mosaic covering was completed (c. 1215-1280).

The real wealth of the atrium mosaics lies in the spiritual message that, with ingenious intuition, assigned them the task of "marking" the time awaiting the coming of Jesus, following the thread that identifies the phases of the story of salvation, after the fall of Man, before his completion in Christ, whose life and mysteries are celebrated in the church mosaics in the interior.

John Ruskin was one of the few art critics that intuited the value and meaning of this message. He defined St Mark's not only as a "place of worship" and "a symbol of the redeemed church of God", but also as "a book of prayer, a miniature parchment on which the Divine Word is written"; indeed, "no city has ever

First small Dome of Joseph.

Second small Dome of Joseph.

Third small Dome of Joseph.

Small Dome of Moses.

Emmanuel Dome.

Saint John the Evangelist Dome with Stories of the Saint.

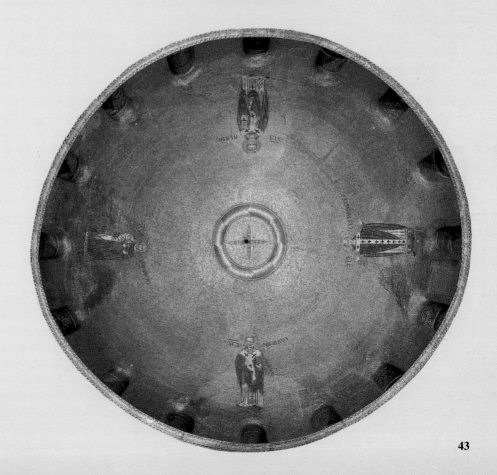

Saint Leonard Dome with the Saints: Leonard (east, Nicholas (south), Clemens (west), Blaise (north).

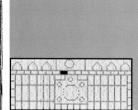

GOLD ALTARPIECE.

The last Supper.
Around a semicircular table Christ is seated
on the left with John resting his head on His
chest, the twelve Apostles and Saint Peter
facing Christ. At the centre of the table,
in profile, Judas pointing to a fish.

Main portal, lower niches.
The Evangelists:
Saint Matthew, Saint Mark,
Saint Luke, Saint John.

had a more glorious Bible" (*The Stones of Venice, V*). Beginning from the southwestern corner, the church decoration narrates an ample tale of the great events of the Old Testament, chosen from the books of Genesis and Exodus. It is continued and developed along the western and northern sides, and is modelled for the most part on the illuminations of the early-Christian Alexandrian (Cotton) Bible (photo pp. 38-39).

The first cupola is that of the Creation, geometrically scanned in three circular bands concentrically encircling a gilded, scaled decoration. The story is subdivided in twenty-six scenes, above which we find the biblical text (in Latin) which begins with the words: "In the beginning God created the heaven and the earth. ...and the spirit of God hovered over the waters." The days of creation follow, each one presenting the figure of God the Creator, identified - according to Eastern ico-

nography - in the young Christ with cruciform halo and cross-staff, the living Word of the Father, and with him, from the beginning, creator of the universe (as can be read at the beginning of the Gospel of John). An angel is placed alongside the creator's work of each day, from one to six. The *benediction of the seventh day* is unusual in the representation of the creation and thus of great interest. In it God, seated on a throne and surrounded, like a sort of regal court, by the six angels of the first six days places his hand in benediction on the seventh angel, the figure of the Sabbath, which he has reserved for himself. Written above are the biblical words: "And God blessed the seventh day."

Next we can observe the *creation of Eve* from Adam's rib, the *temptation of the serpent,* and *the progenitors' disobedience* to God's command and their *banishment from the earthly Para-*

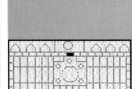

GOLD ALTARPIECE

Crucifixion.
A large Cross with the Greek inscription "Jesus
Christ": Christ nailed to the Cross with blood
spurting to the left on the side of the Virgin, staring at
Him, and on the opposite side Saint John.

dise. In this last scene, a cross stands out very clearly between the trees of paradise, which Adam and Eve must leave, representing an instrument of the redemption promised to all men through God's infinite mercy. The biblical story continues on the surrounding arches and lunettes, near the door of St Clement, with the *birth of Cain and Abel,* and *Cain's crime*, the beginning of an evil that will spread among men until their total destruction by the flood. Only the righteous Noah, his family, and the animals chosen by him will be saved. "But after Noah's death the people said: "Come let us build a city, and a tower, with its top touching heaven" (Genesis 11.4). These words are written above the mosaic that reveals, against the background of a crenellated city, the construction of a brick tower, around which one can observe the feverish activity of the masons who are carrying out the orders of the overseer placed in the centre. The scene, which realistically recalls the activity of a thirteenth-century Venetian building site, is flanked by a second where in front of the unfinished tower, the creator, descended from heaven with his angelic court, has scattered in four directions, confusing their languages, the men who arrogantly thought to realize a kingdom founded on human power alone that could grant ascent to heaven.

After this moment of sin the atrium itinerary continues immediately in the dome and lunette near of the door of St Peter, which narrates the stories of Abraham, progenitor of descendants chosen by God to be saved and initiator of a new story of humanity. Abraham does not take himself into account, but listens docilely to God. The scene of Abraham conversing with God, portrayed by a hand emerging from a strip of sky, is repeated four times and scans the sequence of the story in four parts.

The next three small cupolas in the northern side of the atrium are occupied by the stories of Joseph, the Jew, interpreter of dreams and righteous sufferer. After being sold by his brothers and unjustly condemned by the Egyptians, he enters into the Pharaoh's grace and becomes the saviour of the Egyptian people and of his own brothers, who had betrayed him.

The atrium decoration concludes in the splendour of the small cupola of Moses. Here the scenes follow uninterrupted, rich in figures that are no longer individually silhouetted against the gold but inserted into articulated natural spaces and sumptuous architecture. Here we find the story of Moses, who, saved from the Nile, becomes the saviour and the leader of his people through the desert and across the Red sea towards the promised land. Moses, like Abraham and Joseph before him, is the figure of Jesus, Saviour of all men.

Every scene of this "glorious Bible", immersed in the luminosity of gold tiles, is enriched and completed by a literary text. The Latin texts, written in an epigraphic and abbreviated form that is

The interior of the
basilica.
Central nave and
presbytery.

(p. 48-49)
View of the mosaics
towards the south transept.

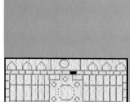

GOLD ALTARPIECE

Descent to Limbo.
Christ with a double Cross raises Adam from the tomb
together with Eve; on the other side
prophets David and Solomon and
Saint John the Baptist can be seen.

absolutely impossible for the majority of the faithful and present day visitors to read for various reasons, are for the most part from the Latin Vulgate. At times, very beautiful prayers and invocations are written on the fronts of the arches, in the half-calottes, and the vaults. They are medieval poems, in Leonine verse, composed for the Venice basilica. We suggest reading a few of the more accessible ones here in the atrium.

Around the entrance to the church, we find the highly visible four Evangelists - Matthew, Mark, Luke and John, in canonical order - inside four preciously decorated niches. They belong to the most ancient mosaics, perhaps done in the late-eleventh century before the construction of the atrium, when the great portal was the exterior entrance to the church. They are held to be works of "Greek" mosaicists (here Greek refers generically to provenance from the Byzantine area) and are mentioned in the ancient Venetian chronicles. *Ecclesiae Christi vigiles/ sunt quattuor isti/ quorum dulce melos/sonat et movet undique coelos* - these are the four "sentinels" of the church of Christ, their sweet song resounds and travels from every part of heaven (photo pp. 44-45). These words, distributed in four hemistichs in each niche, well-express the function that the evangelists, singers of the Word of God, take on here as the "custodians" of the basilica.

On the nearby pendentives of the "well", the space between the exterior portal and the church, the four evangelists are repeated in mosaics that were executed at a much later date. Here the inscriptions, written in a refined linguistic play of rhyme and internal assonance with the name of each of the evangelists (which is lost in translation), are meant to express an individual prayer: *Ablue cuncta reae/ mentis mala sancte Mattheae* - St Matthew, purifies all the guilt of the wicked soul: *Sis nobis Marce/ coelesti gratus in arce* - Oh Mark, be benevolent with us from heaven; *Quo lucet Lucas/ nos Christe piissime ducas* - Oh most pius Christ, lead us to where Luke shines; *Quo sine fine manes/ nos perduc virgo Joannes* - Oh virgin John, lead us to where you rest in eternity. In this central space of the atrium, on the front of the large half-calotte above the door, a prayer is made directly to the evangelist and patron of the city: *Alapis Marce delicta precantibus arce/ ut surgant per to factore suo miserante* - Oh Mark, dismiss the sins of those that pray to you with joined hands, through your intercession and the mercy of God may they be saved". This prayer is directed to the very beautiful St Mark depicted in in liturgical robes in the half-calotte (done by the Zuccato brothers on a cartoon that is perhaps by Titian, 1545).

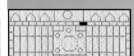

*The devout women at the Sepulchre.
An angel shows the Sepulchre to the
devout women who carry vases
with ointments and incense.*

INTERIOR MOSAICS

Following the preparation and expectation, read in the mosaics of the atrium, we enter the church, the symbolic "promised land" of Abraham and the ancient patriarchs.

The lunette above the main door (photo p .20) immediately suggests a further and more precise key to understanding the space in which we find ourselves. The three figures recall the classical formation of a *Deesis*, the prayer of intercession that, in Eastern iconography shows the Virgin Mother and John the Baptist, humanity's two great intercessors, at the sides of Christ Pantocrator. Here the *Deesis* is interpreted liberally: John the Baptist is replaced by St Mark, patron of the church and city. The words of the gospel (John: Chapter 10) are written on the open book in Jesus's hand: *"Ego sum ostium per me si quis introierit salvabitur et pasqua inveniet* - I am the gate; whoever enters through me will be saved: and will find the pasture of salvation".* These words help us recover forgotten meanings and values: the true "gate" that leads to salvation is Christ himself, his Word communicated to us through his life. Indeed the mosaics of all the domes, vaults, and walls should be read like an illuminated gospel, all of which is gathered together in the evocative luminosity of the golden tiles. In medieval tradition this gilded light, as we have seen, takes on the symbolic meaning of the light of God himself, according to the theology of the Gospel of John, where Jesus says of himself: "I am the light of the world" (8.12).

We are indebted to the well-ordered mind of a medieval theologian for the lines of the iconographic program of the interior mosaics, which are inspired by the canons of

The presbytery complex, with rood screen and high altar seen from the transept.
At the sides of the stairs, windows illuminate the crypt.

Presbytery with the ciborium, sustained by sculpted columns, and the Gold Altarpiece.

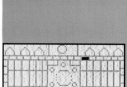

*Incredulity of Saint Thomas.
Christ in front of the closed door invites Thomas
to touch his wounds, surrounded by Saint
Peter, Saint Paul and the Apostles.*

Byzantine art and, for the most part, were realized over the course of the twelfth century. The central nucleus, which narrates the story of Christian salvation, soars from the Messianic prophecies, to the second coming of Christ the Judge, to the end of the world, and has its focal points in the three large domes of the main nave. It should be 'read' from the presbytery towards the facade, from East to West, following the course of the sun, which is symbolically associated with Christ, a sun that never sets for mankind.

The journey through the story of salvation begins in the presbytery dome (photo p. 40) with the coming of the Messiah announced by the prophets who, gathered around the Virgin, show the texts of their prophecies. Mary is found praying in the centre, while, nearby, Isaiah pointing to the beardless youth in the centre of the dome, pronounces the words: "Behold, the Virgin shall conceive, and bear a son, and shall name him Emmanuel" (7.14). David, head of the royal House of Israel, who wears the sumptuous garments of the emperor of Byzantium, proclaims the sovereignty of the child to whom she will give birth: "The fruit of thy body will I set upon thy throne" (Psalms 132.11). The same iconographic theme is repeated on the walls of the central nave: here ten, splendid thirteenth-century mosaic works (the *pinakes*) present the Virgin (on the right wall) and Christ Emmanuel (on the left), encircled respectively by four prophets (photo pp. 64-65).

The fulfilment of the prophecy begins in the scenes that portray the *angel's annunciation to Mary, the adoration of the Magi, the presentation in the temple,* and *the baptism of Jesus in the River Jordan* (photo p 51) on the vault above the rood screen. These mosaics were redone on cartoons by Jacopo Tintoretto in the late-sixteenth century, after the older cycle was ruined and destroyed.

Another medieval execution of the *baptism of Jesus*, located inside the baptistry, recalls the great wealth of the motifs of Byzantine icons: Christ is nude and covered by the waters of the Jordan, almost a symbol of the shroud that was to cover him after his death. At his right John the Baptist pours water over him; at his left three angels are bent in adoration. The dove of the Holy Spirit descends upon his head from the open sky.

The acts of Jesus - comforting the sick, the suffering, and sinners - are translated into numerous images on the walls and the vaults of the two transepts.

The south and west vaults under the central dome gather together the conclusive episodes of his life: *entrance into Jerusalem* (photo pp. 48-49), *the last supper, the washing of the feet, the kiss of Judas, and Pilate's sentence.*

The large panel of the *prayer in the garden* of the south wall was added in the thirteenth century and constitutes one of the masterpieces of all the mosaics (photo p. 33). Jesus' suffering and the indifference of his friends are narrated in three successive scenes, dominated by a rocky landscape, in which flowers and trees of extraordinary beauty sprout forth.

Scenes of *the crucifixion, the descent into limbo (the anastasis)* with the great figure of Christ victorious over death and *the resurrection* are illustrated in the centre of the basilica. The great dome, at the intersection of the transept, celebrates the final mystery of the life of Jesus: *the Ascension into heaven* (photo p. 41). In the star-studded central circle, Christ, seated on a rainbow, is carried upwards by four angels in flight. Below the three very beautiful trees of multiform foliage that represent the earthly reality, the twelve apostles with the Virgin and two angels, depicted in lifelike poses, take part in the mystery of which they will become testimony. Between the small openings, six-

*All around View of the Mosaics
towards the North Transept.*

teen female figures in a dancing sequence personify the virtues and beatitudes: among them are faith, justice, patience, mercy, and, the most noble of all, charity, crowned and in royal garb "the mother of all the virtues" as the surrounding inscription suggests.

The third cupola is that of the Pentecost, where the Holy Spirit (centre) in the symbol of the dove descends upon the Apostles in tongues of fire (photo p. 42). At the base, between the small openings, pairs of all peoples listen, each in their own language, to the message of love directed to them, as narrated in the Acts of the Apostles. These are the variegated peoples of the earth that reach Venice from every corner of the world, their languages resounding under the basilica's golden domes. Indeed for almost one thousand years, the basilica of St Mark's has communicated to everyone in the language of its mosaics the great message of the Christian faith rooted in the very tradition of the city of Venice.

56

GOLD ALTARPIECE

ENTRANCE INTO JERUSALEM.
Christ riding a donkey followed by Peter and
John. Outside the town gate of Jerusalem the
crowd throngs, from a tree a child scatters
leaves, two other children stretch clothes and
scatter leaves on the ground.

GOLD ALTARPIECE

DESCENT TO LIMBO.
Christ with the Cross rises from the broken
Gates of Hell, with one hand he raises Adam
next to whom is Eve, while from the opposite
side David, Solomon and Saint John the
Baptist look on.

58

GOLD ALTARPIECE

CRUCIFIXION.
Christ is nailed to the Cross with the inscription "Crucifixion"; on the left Mary and the devout women; on the right Saint John and Saint Longinus, a Roman centurion. The windows symbolize the town of Jerusalem.

GOLD ALTARPIECE

ASCENSION.
Christ ascends to heaven carried by two angels in a mandorla; below, in the centre, there is the inscription "Ascension"; lower, the Virgin and, on the two sides, two groups of six Apostles each, led by Peter on the right and Paul on the left.

GOLD ALTARPIECE

PENTECOST.
The twelve Apostles form an oval figure. The space in front, delimited by an arch, is occupied by two kings, a black one and a white one. Peter and Paul are sitting in the front row. The Holy Ghost descends upon them in the form of tongues of fire.

GOLD ALTARPIECE

"DORMITIO VIRGINIS".
The Virgin Mary lies on her death bed and is surrounded by Saint Peter, Saint Paul and the Apostles. The figure of Christ holds in his arms the soul of the Virgin, portrayed by a child, while it is being carried to heaven.

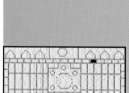

GOLD ALTARPIECE

Ascension.
Christ is carried to Heaven in a mandorla
by two angels; below in the centre the Virgin
between two groups of Apostles with Saint
Peter on the left and Saint Paul on the right.

(p. 56-58)
The Pala d'Oro. Lower part.

Right nave.
Mosaic in
opus tessellatum.
The exact placing
of this mosaic
is shown at no. 2
of the plan
of the mosaics
on page 22.

PALA D'ORO

Framed within the ancient ciborium in the sacred space of the presbytery, the Pala d'Oro faces the faithful, who follow the liturgy from the nave, in a blaze of pure light amidst flashes of gold and reflections of pearls and precious stones. This luminosity, symbol of divine light, is created by the *cloisonné* enamel decoration of the panels, entirely realized in Byzantium between the tenth and twelfth centuries. On each sheet of gold, inside the sometimes incredibly minute alveoli (*cloisons*), which define the design, a very thin layer of vitreous paste in different colours allows the gold of the background to shine through. The Pala (altarpiece) took on its present form more than six centuries ago, when Doge Andrea Dandolo, in 1343,

commissioned Giambattista Bonesegna to make the Gothic frame (3.34 x 2.51 m.) in gilded silver, studded with approximately two thousand precious and semi-precious gems, within which more ancient enamels are set. The two inscriptions at the base narrate the story of the Pala, which had two precedents: one under the rule of Ordelaffo Falier (doge, 1102-1118); the other under Pietro Ziani (doge, 1205-1229). The latter was composed after the large panels were transported to Venice from the church of the *Pantocrator* in Constantinople, conquered in 1204. They now form the upper part of the present Pala, including the six squares, with the "holidays" of the Byzantine church, placed at the sides of the Archangel Michael (from the left: *entrance into Jerusalem, the resurrection, the crucifixion, the Ascension, the descent of the Holy Spirit,* and *the death of the Virgin or dormitio Virginis,* photo pp. 59-61).

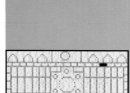

Pentecost.
The rays of Wisdom descend from above upon the twelve Apostles
sitting at an oval table, with Saints Paul and Peter in the centre.
In the front of the table are standing two kings, a white one
and a black one. The latter are meant to
symbolize that the Gospel will be preached to all mankind.

The entire lower part, the enamelled panels of which were surely commissioned by Venice from Byzantine artists (photo pp. 56-58), appears to be the city of which St John speaks in Revelations (chapter 21): The angel … "showed me the Holy City, Jerusalem, descending from God in heaven and shining with the glory of God. Its splendour is like that of a very precious jewel… The wall are made of jasper, and the city of pure gold, similar to clear crystal. The foundations of the city walls are decorated with every kind of precious stone."

The figure of Christ, the Pantocrator, Lord of the universe, sits in the centre on a jewelled throne; his right hand is raised in a gesture of benediction, his left holds the open Book decorated with precious stones that express the inestimable value of his announcement. Each of the four evangelists gathered around him is writing his own gospel. Directly below the figure of Christ we find his mother, the Virgin Mary, in the act of praying; at her sides are the two donors, Doge Ordelaffo Falier and Empress Irene. Depicted above the figure of Christ between two cherubs and two archangels is the *hetimasia*, or the preparation of the throne of the last judgement. At the sides of the central composition, placed in a hierarchicals order from the bottom up, are twelve prophets, twelve apostles, and twelve

Left lateral nave.
Jesus blessing among four Prophets.
(From left to right) Hosea, Joel, Jesus, Micah, Jeremiah.

archangels. The latter accent the gesture of adoration, their bodies bowing increasing forward as they move inward.

Aligned above and enclosed between deacons spreading incense, one finds almost all the "holidays" of the Byzantine church (the *dormitio Virginis* is missing): from the left, *the annunciation, nativity, the presentation in the temple, the baptism of Jesus, the last supper, the crucifixion, the descent into Limbo, the resurrection, the incredulity of Thomas, the Ascension, the Pentecost* (photos pp. 26, 30, 32, 36, 44, 46, 50, 52, 54, 62, 64).

The ten small squares at the sides represent, vertically, on the left, the salient episodes in the life of St Mark (photo pp. 4, 6, 8, 10, 12) and, on the right, the episodes regarding his martyrdom in Alexandria, Egypt and the translation of his body to Venice (photo pp. 16, 18, 20, 22, 24). Numerous round enamelled plaques of various dimensions, which portray the half-busts of the saints venerated by the Venetians, complete this grand and precious altarpiece.

At the centre of the presbytery the Pala d'Oro repeats and summarizes the very message the Venetian basilica proposes to faithful followers and visitors: it is not only a theological, but also a devotional and political "summa", where St Mark's fundamental presence gives meaning to the many levels of decoration (works in mosaics, marble, bronze, and wooden marquetry) and allows one to intuit the precise will of those who continued to commission these art works in eras very distant one from another.

The Pala d'Oro was originally turned towards the apse on weekdays and in the absence of liturgical celebrations, and it has only been more generally visible in the past few decades. In ancient times it was fixed and, when it was not to be seen, it was covered by one of the altarpieces known as "feriali" (week day). The most ancient and the most beautiful is the Pala Feriale by Paolo Veneziano, the first great Venetian painter of fourteenth century, who was commissioned by Doge Andrea Dandolo, at the same time the present Gothic cornice of the Pala d'Oro was realized. Now conserved in the museum, the Pala Feriale is an extraordinary panel painting, realized on two registers. The upper one depicts the figure of Christ deposed from the cross flanked on the right by the Virgin, St Mark, and St Theodore, and on the left by St John the Evangelist, St Peter, and St Nicholas. The gilded background, of clearly Byzantine taste, wraps, in a celestial atmosphere, the figures realized with a new spatial sensitivity, evident in the scenes with the seven stories of St Mark that occupy the lower register and repeat episodes already represented in the plaques of the Pala d'Oro and elsewhere in the basilica.

Right lateral nave.
The Virgin praying among four Prophets.
(From left to right) Isaiah, David, The Virgin, Solomon, Ezekiel.

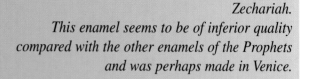

GOLD ALTARPIECE

Zechariah.
This enamel seems to be of inferior quality
compared with the other enamels of the Prophets
and was perhaps made in Venice.

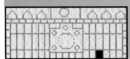

BAPTISTRY

The baptistry occupies the space tin the southern part of the basilica, which in ancient times was part of the atrium and opened towards the quay. The information preceding the realization of the present early-fourteenth century chapel - built on the will of Andrea Dandolo, a highly cultured humanist and friend of Francesco Petrarch, the first procurator of St Mark and later doge (1343-1354) - is highly uncertain. It is based on a few, occasional archaeological finds, such as the frescoes found on the north wall by the overseer Forlati in the 1950s, which depict an Ascension of Jesus and seem to be a part of the decoration of the ancient portico.

Regarding the transformation requested by Dandolo, a few scholars have recently observed that the Doge, in addition to his desire to give the basilica a new baptistry richly decorated with mosaics representing the latest expression of the Venetian-Byzantine school (with a few already Gothic characteristics), wanted the baptistry to celebrate both himself and his family. (This explains his presence as a donor at the foot of a large crucifix). The baptistry was also intended to serve as a funeral chapel and conserves two beautiful Gothic tombs: that of Doge Giovanni Soranzo (+1329) and that of Andrea Dandolo himself, the last doge to be buried in the basilica.

The baptistry, known in Venetian dialect as the "*giesia dei puti*" (the childrens' church), is now accessed

Baptistry.
Saint Mark,
Saint Luke,
Saint John,
Saint Matthew.

The Baptistry
with the baptismal Fonts .

Baptistry. The Magi on their way to Bethlehem.

through the church. Its original entrance from the Piazzetta better identified the three environments into which the chapel is subdivided: the ante-baptistry, where the catechumens awaited the baptismal rite; the baptistry itself; and the presbytery.

The mosaic decoration, which has already been mentioned, covers the upper part of the structure: the walls, the undersides of the arches, the vaults, and cupolas. The wall mosaics develop an ample cycle of scenes with episodes from the life of John the Baptist (from the annunciation of his birth to his father Zacharias, on the lunette to the right of the altar, through his martyrdom under King Herod, on the left lunette). In the area of the ante-baptistry the life of the Baptist meets with episodes of the infancy of Christ, and, in a privileged position, particularly illuminated by the southern light, one finds the very beautiful scene of the baptism of Jesus, of which we have already spoken. One should view the upper part of the mosaics beginning from the vault of the ante-baptistry which gathers together the Messianic annunciation written in the scrolls of the twelve prophets. It continues on the cupola above the baptismal font (the bronze reliefs on the cover were executed by students of Jacopo Sansovino on a mid-16th c. project by this master) that illustrates the mission of the Apostles. The Twelve are depicted in the act of baptizing the different peoples, to whom they have addressed their preaching. At the centre, the full figure of Christ, risen from the dead, pronounces the words of the gospel of Mark: "Go into all the world and preach the good news to all creation. Whoever believes and is baptized will be saved...." (15.15,16). Finally in the heavenly vision of the last cupola the new angelic hierarchy surrounds the Christ in Glory, sustained by Seraphim, while the underlying Crucifix recalls sufferance and death Jesus passed through for the redemption of all mankind.

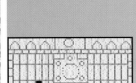

GOLD ALTARPIECE

Daniel.
The figure is outstanding for its brightly coloured vestments and is considered amongst the best of the series of the Twelve Prophets.

CHAPEL OF ST ISIDORE

The small chapel accessed through the northern transept is dedicated to Isidore, the Greek Saint whose remains were brought to Venice from Chios in 1125 by Doge Domenico Michiel. The doges' devotion to this Saint recalls that for St Mark. Isidore lies behind the altar above his sepulchre, watched over by an angel, while the mosaics of the vault celebrate the facts of his life, martyrdom, and translation to Venice. The sculptures and mosaics found here are very valuable works from the mid-fourteenth century, when Doge Andrea Dandolo wanted to realize this chapel in honour of St Isidore (along with the baptistry). The Blessed Sacrament is now preserved in this silent and intense space where weekday liturgies are celebrated.

Vault of the Chapel of St Isidore. The Venetians translating the body of St Isidore from the Island of Chios.

GOLD ALTARPIECE

Ezechiel.
It is a good quality enamel
as may be seen from its position
close to the Pantocrator.

CRYPT

A recent restoration, which sought to make the pavement and walls impermeable, has rendered the crypt fit for use. Underlying the presbytery and the side chapels of St Peter and St Clement, this very ancient space, in which parts of the first church dating back to the ninth century can be identified, houses a small but important central chapel. It is now freed from later overlaying structures, and the rich openly-worked marble transennas of Byzantine craftsmanship are visible. This the precious ancient tomb of St Mark, destination of secular pilgrimages from all over Europe. The Saint's reliquaries have only rested under the refectory table of the high altar in the presbytery since 1835.

Baptistry. Lunette above the door towards the church. Salome's dance and the martyrdom of John the Baptist.

The crypt, after its recent restauration, appears with its rows of columns and its somewhat small size, as the prestigious site which for centuries housed the remains of St Mark.

(pp.72-73) Ascension Dome and Vaults.

(p. 74) The vaults under the Ascension Dome.

(p.75) Saint John Dome, Stories of the Virgin.

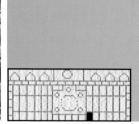

GOLD ALTARPIECE

David.
This is a regal figure owing to the rich garments
(light-blue robe and cloak, red shoes, crown)
and the attitude of serious composure.

SACRISTY

The sacristy can be reached through the chapel of St Peter. It is a vast space on a rectangular plan capped by a high vault and illuminated by three large windows on the wall towards the Rio di Palazzo. It was realized between 1486 and 1493 by the building overseer Giorgio Spavento, along with the adjacent church of St Theodore.

The wall toward the church and those of the sides, up to the fourth arch, are covered with wainscoted seats and benches in carved walnut designed around 1550 by J. Sansovino.

The wooden wainscoting of the second part of the sacristy is of great interest. The carved and inlaid doors of the three large, simply-constructed cupboards frame still lifes, liturgical objects, and musical instruments.

Above their upper shelf there is a decorative panel of inlaid waincot encased in an uninterrupted wooden frame 2.20 m. high. Each of the wainscots, seven for each of the three sides, depicts an urban view, inside a round arch. Some of these views "narrate" episodes from the life of St Mark. These masterpieces of intarsia, which can be dated between 1498 and 1506, were crafted by Antonio and Paolo Mola, two brothers from Mantua, who left their signature on the second and third intarsia on the left.

The mosaics on the upper part of the walls and the vault are of a later date and are sometimes attributed to a project by Titian. They are well inserted and give unity to the Renaissance purity of the architecture. The mosaics themselves were realized between 1524 and 1530 by Alberto Zio, Marco Luciano Rizzo, and Francesco Zuccato. The Christological plan is centred on the vault, dominated by a large cross with Christ and the four evangelists, and continues along the sides and on the lunettes with the prophets, who announced Christ, and the Apostles, who were his worldly testimony. On the western side, the Virgin and Child is flanked by St George and St Theodore. Scholars recognize the mosaics of the vault to be of the highest quality.

Sacristy, ceiling.
Two Details of the Mosaic Decoration.

Ceiling.
The Mosaic Cross.

Jacopo Sansovino. Sacristy Door,
Portraits of contemporary Artists,
symbols of Prophets.

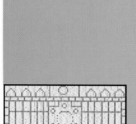

GOLD ALTARPIECE

Habakkuk.
The prophet Habakkuk as the other
Eleven, faces front under an arch, his right
hand blessing and his left holding a scroll.

TREASURY

The treasury of the basilica is still conserved in the ancient rooms between the church and the ducal palace, which are accessed through a door of the south transept enriched by a thirteenth-century mosaic that, in remembrance of the fire of 1231, depicts two angels supporting the reliquary of the Cross miraculously intact.

The small vestibule leads left into the Sanctuary, and, right, into the treasury itself. There are numerous reliquaries in the sanctuary, some of which are very precious – gifts given to Venice by popes or princes, or, in keeping with medieval customs, relics gathered from Constantinople, the Holy Land, or the sanctuaries in the Eastern basin of the Mediterranean.

In the larger room, to the right, 283 pieces of Treasure are gathered together in glass cases. They are very valuable works in gold, silver, rock crystal, glass, and other precious materials, the most ancient nucleus of which is part of the booty transported from Constantinople to Venice after 1204. We can still admire what has remained after the disastrous sacking following the end of the Republic in 1797 and the forced sale of pearls and precious stones between 1815 and 1819 to meet the economic needs of the church restoration.

There are four categories of objects:

- those belonging to Antiquity and the Early Middle Ages, among which are two very beautiful rock (quartz) crystal lamps sculpted in the form of fish and two amphorae with handles in animal forms, each of which is carved from a single block of precious Eastern agate;

- those of Byzantine goldsmithery from around the year 1000: chalices and patens in semi-precious stones with silver and gold frames decorated with cloisonné enamels, which can also be found in the two portable icons with the image of St Michael Archangel;

- a few belonging to Islamic art (9-10th c.), in particular the splendid goblet in turquoise glass with stylized animals in relief framed in gilded silver set with semi-precious stones;

- those of Western provenance and craftsmanship, including the famous perfume burner in the form of a small building on a central plan topped by five cupolas (reproduced here) and many other pieces of especially fine filigree craftsmanship, known as "*opus venetum ad filum*".

Other objects worthy of observation include the two altarpieces on the south wall: the one belonging to the basilica and dedicated to St Mark (late-13th c.) is still used today to cover the high altar for important holidays; the other (15th c.), a gift of Pope Gregory XII, is from the cathedral church of S. Pietro di Castello.

The last precious object is St Mark's reliquary-throne in calcareous alabaster of Alexandrian craftsmanship (perhaps 6th c.), which was a gift of emperor Heraclius to the patriarch Primigenius of Grado in 630. The symbols of the four Evangelists can be read on the sides; the back depicts the lamb under a tree from which flow the four rivers of Paradise according to a vision of the Apocalypse.

MARCIANO MUSEUM

The Marciano Museum is accessed from the atrium through a small door to the right of the main entrance and a steep stairway that leads to the level of the women's galleries. The rooms of the museum are distributed on the sides towards the quay at the south and the small square of the Leoncini on the north.

The most important objects presently displayed include:

- the Horses of St Mark, the classical quadriga, on whose origins scholars are still divided between Roman and Greek craftsmanship (placed here to protect them from atmospheric pollution after the 1970s restoration that brought them back to their ancient splendour);

- the Pala Feriale by Paolo Veneziano and his sons Luca and Giovanni (see p. 65);

- numerous mosaic fragments from, above all, the baptistry (14th c.);

- valuable Persian rugs from the seventeenth century ;

- liturgical vestments with very refined Burano lace finishing (17th and 18th c.);

- miniature choir books from the fifteenth, sixteenth, and seventeenth centuries (much of what remains of the great heritage of the basilica's books of liturgy are now in the Marciana library, though some have been lost).

From the rooms of the Treasury one can also access the women's galleries, under the vault of the Paradise, from where there is a very beautiful view of the basilica's interior and a close up of the dome and vault mosaics. From here one can also reach the basilica loggia, from which one dominates the square and, on the south side, the Piazzetta with a splendid view of the islands of San Giorgio and the Giudecca.

Treasury,
Perfume Burner
(gilded silver, 10th century).

Marciano Museum.
Covering of the Gold Altarpiece.
Translation of Saint Mark's body (detail).

(P. 80) The Madonna Nicopeia.
Byzantine icon from Constantinople.